YOU CAN HANDLE CONFLICT: HANDS ↑ OR ↓ WORDS?

Do you ever wish you could change a story or choose a different ending?

IN THESE BOOKS, YOU CAN!
Read along and when you see this:

WHAT HAPPENS NEXT?

Skip to the page for that choice, and see what happens.

In this story, Quinn wants the swing Aidan is using. Will she use her hands or her words? YOU make the choices!

It's time for recess! Quinn has been waiting all morning to swing. She runs fast, but Aidan takes the last swing. Quinn is angry!

WHAT HAPPENS NEXT?

If Quinn grabs the swing from Aidan, turn the page.
If Quinn asks for a turn, turn to page 22.

Quinn pulls the swing out of Aidan's hands. "Hey!" Aidan says. "I had the swing first! Give it back!"

WHAT HAPPENS NEXT?

If Quinn pushes Aidan away, turn to page 6.
If Quinn gives the swing back, turn to page 20.

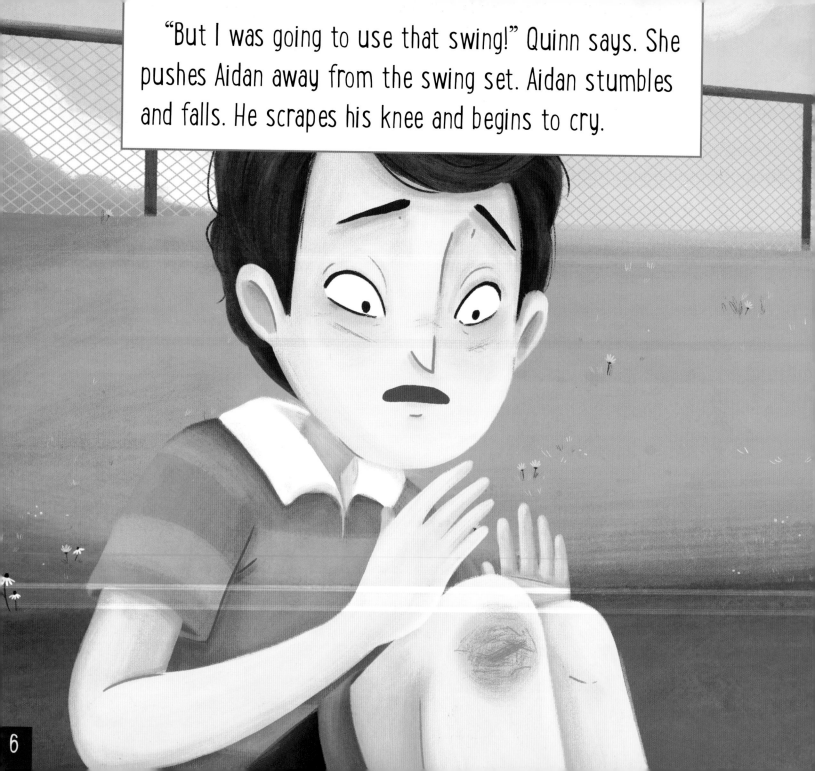

"But I was going to use that swing!" Quinn says. She pushes Aidan away from the swing set. Aidan stumbles and falls. He scrapes his knee and begins to cry.

6

WHAT HAPPENS NEXT?

→ If Quinn gets on the swing, turn the page.
If Quinn says she's sorry, turn to page 18. ←

Mr. Tim rushes over. "What happened, Aidan?" he asks.
"Quinn took my swing and pushed me down!" Aidan says.
Mr. Tim turns to Quinn. "Please come talk to us, Quinn," he says.

WHAT HAPPENS NEXT?

→ If Quinn keeps swinging and ignores Mr. Tim, turn the page.
If Quinn stops to talk, turn to page 14. ←

Mr. Tim is upset. "Quinn, please get off the swing and come with me."

"*Uh-oh,*" she thinks. "*I'm in trouble.*"

TURN THE PAGE →

Mr. Tim takes Quinn to the principal, Ms. Ortiz. Ms. Ortiz says, "I'm disappointed in you, Quinn. You will sit inside during recess all week. You also will write apology notes to Aidan and Mr. Tim."

Quinn feels bad. She should have used her words instead of her hands.

THE END

Go to page 23.

Quinn looks at Mr. Tim's face. She realizes that she has been selfish and has hurt her friend. "I'm sorry," Quinn says. She helps Aidan up.

TURN THE PAGE →

"Thank you for apologizing, Quinn," says Mr. Tim, "but you will need to sit out for the rest of recess." Quinn is sad, but she knows this is fair. She should not have put her hands on Aidan.

THE END

⤷ Go to page 23. ←

Quinn sees Aidan's bloody knee. She feels bad.
"I'm sorry, Aidan. Let me help you up," Quinn says.
She walks him to the nurse's office to get a bandage.
She doesn't get to swing before recess is over. She knows
that she should not have put her hands on Aidan.

THE END

→ Go to page 23. ←

Quinn stops and thinks. She puts her hands down. "Sorry, Aidan," she says. "Can I have a turn on the swing when you are done?"
Aidan calms down, too. "Okay," he says.

Quinn calmed down and used her words. Both kids get a turn with the swing.

THE END

→ Go to page 23. ←

Quinn slows down. "Hey, Aidan," she says.
"Can I have a turn when you are done?"
"Sure!" Aidan replies.
Both kids have fun playing until recess is over.

THE END

THINK AGAIN

- What happened at the end of the path you chose?
- Did you like that ending?
- Go back to page 3. Read the story again and pick different choices. How did the story change?

We are all free to make choices, but choices have consequences. What would YOU do if something like this happened to you?

With love to Aidan and Quinn, two kiddos
who have plenty of words.—C.C.M.

AMICUS ILLUSTRATED and AMICUS INK
are published by Amicus
P.O. Box 1329, Mankato, MN 56002
www.amicuspublishing.us

Library of Congress Cataloging-in-Publication Data
Names: Miller, Connie Colwell, 1976- author. | Assanelli, Victoria, 1984- illustrator.
Title: You can handle conflict : hands or words? / by Connie Colwell Miller ;
    illustrated by Victoria Assanelli.
Description: Mankato, Minnesota : Amicus, [2018] | Series: Making good choices
Identifiers: LCCN 2017004927 (print) | LCCN 2017009556 (ebook) |
    ISBN 9781681511627 (library binding) | ISBN 9781681512525 (ebook) |
    ISBN 9781681522319 (pbk.)
Subjects: LCSH: Interpersonal conflict in children—Juvenile literature. |
    Decision making in children—Juvenile literature.
Classification: LCC BF723.I645 M55 2018 (print) | LCC BF723.I645 (ebook) |
    DDC 155.4/192—dc23
LC record available at https://lccn.loc.gov/2017004927

Editor: Rebecca Glaser
Designer: Kathleen Petelinsek

Printed in China
HC   10 9 8 7 6 5 4 3 2 1
PB   10 9 8 7 6 5 4 3 2 1

ABOUT THE AUTHOR

Connie Colwell Miller is a writer, editor, and instructor who lives in Mankato, Minnesota, with her four children. She has written over 80 books for young children. She likes to tell stories to her kids to teach them important life lessons.

ABOUT THE ILLUSTRATOR

Victoria Assanelli was born during the autumn of 1984 in Buenos Aires, Argentina. She spent most of her childhood playing with her grandparents, reading books, and drawing doodles. She began working as an illustrator in 2007, and has illustrated several textbooks and storybooks since.